Cazique

Cazique

Matthew Clegg

Longbarrow Press

Published in 2018 by
Longbarrow Press
76 Holme Lane
Sheffield
S6 4JW

www.longbarrowpress.com

Printed by T.J. International Ltd,
Padstow, Cornwall

The jacket design incorporates the banknote created by Gregor MacGregor and 'issued' by the fictitious Bank of Poyais in the 1820s. Reproduced courtesy of the National Numismatic Collection, National Museum of American History at the Smithsonian Institution.

ISBN 978-1-906175-35-1

First edition

Contents

Officer / Zipped File

Holodets

Cazique

Officer / Zipped File

'Everything that you must now experience as an officer, my dear Herr Kappus, would have struck you in just the same way in any of the existing professions; and even had you been without position and had, independently, sought free and individual social relationships, you would still not have been spared this feeling of constraint.'

Rainer Maria Rilke, *Letters to a Young Poet*,
translated by Stephen Cohn

"The poet said: 'this is the miserable fate
Of wretched souls deserving neither
Praise nor blame but mere indifference.'"

Dante, *Inferno*, translated by Sean O'Brien

'Inside its cocoon of work or social obligation, the human spirit slumbers for the most part, registering the distinction between pleasure and pain, but not nearly as alert as we pretend.'

E.M. Forster, *A Passage to India*

#1 The Action Plan

The officer was not returning calls.
He was progressing the action plan.
The officer was squatting on his mails
because he knew he was the wrong man
for yet another job. The officer
was reformatting the action plan
for the fifth time. The previous officer
had drawn up a draft. This new version
would be the most cogent strategy so far.
The officer was reminded to set down
achievable outcomes. The greatest care
must be taken. Ticking off each milestone
would get in the way, he knew, of the good idea
when it materialised from elsewhere.

~13

Late afternoon train.
The passenger to his right
opens a man bag
and vomits into its girth.
He zips up, and hugs it tight.

#2 His Team Leader

Wants to suggest he might not encounter
problems with his Local Authority clients
were he dressed more formally. If he casts
his eyes about him he is sure to find
many fine examples of what to wear.
Her arm trembles as she picks up her pen.
But no… He no longer desires to argue
about such things. He knows, too well,
it would demand more time than she has.
He is not above wearing jacket and tie
if they would make the policies seem
more credible to those inclined to argue.
He no longer wishes to deceive himself
that such possibilities can be ignored.

~12

Having her manicure
the woman in the salon
surveys window glare.
She melts into an oyster
of pure selfwhere, elsewhere, gone.

#3 When Delivering Difficult Messages

The consultant has the following advice:
Don't fidget. Don't make free with your body.
Hold your audience, as if in a vice,
with your gaze. Keep your tone steady
to the final destination of the known.
Bullet-point your parameters beforehand
and don't digress, never improvise, even
when your client doesn't seem to understand.
Don't be conscripted. Joining them in doubt
is a sign of weakness you don't need
to indulge. By all means, help them out,
but make them ask before you concede.
The result we're aiming for, guys, is closure
and saying least is always, always more.

~11

Mooning between trains
on the bridge spanning platforms
he counts sly spiders
absilking down the lamplight
to stitch the rims of their webs.

#4 Policy

He's holding forth as he's been trained to do.
He has the facts. The charts. He's in the know.
The policy he's quoting is perfectly clear.
This is the inside view you're party to.
He shows no signs of lapsing from the script.
You are drawn in despite the doubts you have.
He slowly steels his tone with his advance
to cow the nerve of any who dissent.
This version of events has been approved
by those who've had the time to think it through.
He has to say there's something slightly dense
about the need to question this at all.
He huddles up with colleagues later on.
All that can be done, now, they have done.

~10

In his MP3
bubble, on the shopping mall
up escalator,
he looks skywards at hailstones
rapping hate mail against glass.

#5 Between Train and Tram Stop

He walks through bus station and subway
turning down vagrants pleading for change.
On the wet pavement, amongst chip trays
and melanomas of gum, a busker
hams the blues on a busted guitar.
He gives him nothing. Climbing the steps
by the multi-storey car park, he feels
like the city is about to break into song,
but clams up as soon as he halts to listen.
He wants to belong. Stopped by a beggar
he caves in a tiny scrap of his wage.
A woman calls him a mug, shouts after
the beggar, *what's wrong with working?*
as if the question requires no response.

~9

Outside Walkabout
at 7 a.m., he spies
a lesser redpoll
logging edibles against
gritstones, peck by ticking peck.

#6 The Company Man

Asks him to sit down and brace himself.
The paper he composed for them last week
was not so well received. *Let me be frank.*
The vision you project is not our own.
The issues you make problems are best seen
as challenges to rise to and enjoy.
I sense that you are not quite hearing me,
or harbouring resentment: is this true?
Back home he drinks a bottle of cheap red,
sleeps in fits and starts. When morning comes
the station is amok with drowsy wasps.
He rubs his eyes and studies waves of torque
revealed as sunlight catches glass. What else?
The grit in his coffee. The clamp in his chest.

~8

The entitlement
of senior executives
in passenger aisles
can be measured by how long
they prepare for sitting down.

#7 A Crash is Coming

I know a crash is coming to me.
I've stood on the brink of it for years.
Sometimes I think the crash is me.

Tight in my skin, late in the city
I weave a ballet through passing cars.
I know a crash is coming to me,

taking shape in all I strive to be.
My breath is shallow, my pulse careers.
Sometimes I think the crash is me.

Adrenaline swells in every artery;
it's pushed each lover I've had to tears.
I know a crash is coming to me –

if I don't go home I might break free
from what stalks me through the sleepless hours.
Sometimes I think the crash is me.

Fear of fear is what contains me
and I fear that more than all my fears.
I know a crash is coming to me.
Sometimes I think the crash is me.

~7

A coal-black beetle
concentrates its gloss against
a bleaching pavement.
It anticipates the rush,
still waiting to be impressed.

#8 Disciplinary Report

It came to our attention, recently,
that the officer has been slandering
our chair. This is no more than hearsay –
the source the chair himself is quoting
refuses to bear witness on the case.
Still the process has been carried through.
We cannot let our chair lose this much face:
by proxy, it reflects upon us too.
The officer has also expressed 'views'
that set a bad example, in the main.
He admitted to this point in interview,
but seems no more repentant than before.
Although our charges couldn't be sustained
we reminded him how serious they were.

~6

Into the car park
under B&M Bargains
snowflakes ebb and gust.
Through a grate in the ceiling
a spindrift of failing light.

#9 His Team Leader

Has been briefing him on ownership
and projecting their values with confidence;
and asks him to consider if his 'illness'
might have something to do with the fact
he can't drive. It is his role to accept
that this is not beyond the pale, and no insult
to intelligence, but were he driving
he would not be able to walk out
after this interminable meeting
and embrace a sense of something other
watching snowflakes swirl like ghosts
of lost comets around one steadfast
lamp post. He finds no allusion to this
in his *Behavioural Competencies.*

~5

5 a.m. commute.
The bald zero on his scalp
tightens in the chill.
An owl grips the rose of light
fizzing around a streetlamp.

#10 Think Positive

This is how it will be in a year, he says –
Nina Simone's *Feeling Good* in his head;
the big swing band bursting in like God
or a new pay scale. Think positive, he says.
The on-time train advances without delay.
He has the laptop out, the mobile on.
A swift keeps pace with the speeding train
then catches the sun before twisting away.
Perfect. So perfect he could be dreaming.
Precisely. Thinking a thing doesn't make it so,
or wanting it. He can see it clearly now.
He'll walk right in to chair the meeting
and the music, the swift, the sun – whatever –
none of it will touch on the agenda.

-4

The shorter emails;
the long intervals between;
the greater turning
to professional concerns:
in these stages, friendship thins.

#11 The Realities

He tries to keep his mind on the job
and let the job be enough for his mind.
Why, with him, is that always a problem?
He wants someone to say his question
is a good one. Life keeps sending him
secret messages: a code of black mould
on his bedroom wall; a heat mirage
above a standing train. What good is his mind?
It's a bluebottle shut inside a fridge.
Reality scratches through, but like noise
leaking from someone else's headphones.
He can't pin it down or quite blot it out.
The hornet he found crawling in his sheets
prevents him, now, from thinking of much else.

~3

It is standing room
only on the slow train home.
The drunk behind him
is bleeding from his hairline
and is hungry for contact.

#12 Report for Management Team

He comes home wrecked and highly strung.
Several briefings with management team
have not revealed where he's going wrong.
He's unable, as yet, to ascertain
which views are acceptable to express.
The directorate seem increasingly irate.
He tries to imagine his report a success.
It will be the famous, groundbreaking report
that reminds everyone why they are here.
Although he manages, at length, to sleep
he's haunted by a recurring dream, where
he stands before the panel, unprepared,
stammering his report on an endless loop
and pinched, fish-like faces blink and stare.

-2

His fledgling efforts
are a subject of critique
amongst his colleagues.
'Neither here nor there', they say;
neither help nor harm themselves.

#13 Performance Appraisal

About half way he feels himself clam up.
There is no more that he can think to say
that seems the sort of thing he's meant to say
or not, at least, the kind he knows he's not.
His manager informs him in her way
that she intends to be much more severe.
There are, she says, no reasons she can see
why the targets they assigned should not be met.
There is no more to say that's not been said.
He asks if he must still go through with this
if he concedes an impasse and resigns.
It seems there is no way to cut this short.
She asks him to go home and think again.
They follow the agenda to the end.

Zipped File: ~1

On the seventh floor
of a glass-fronted stairwell,
forty-eight flies, dead:
each one butted the sunlight
and buzzed still under neon.

Holodets

'Holodets is a traditional Russian meal which is served during various celebrations. The word holodets derives from the Russian word "holod" meaning "cold".'

http://bridgetomoscow.com

'Love, religion, and politics form the argument, and are as much the cause of quarrels now as they were then.'

Thomas Medwin's *Journal of the Conversations of Lord Byron*

'Is it only right that a poet is restrained and proper?'

Catullus, translated by Daisy Dunn

Muse

after Pushkin

She loved me when my scalp was thick with hair.

She leased me the flute with seven cylinders,

and loaned me her eye. I still had my health,
so up and down that singeing scale of breath

I modelled tunes with grubby fingers.
The jigs and reels of jobbing ceilidh players

were fused with hymns fuguing to the God.
Sun and Earth waltzed as I dossed in the shade

tuning my ear to the elusive Colleen.
She tossed me scraps if I fluked her theme,

or flicking her fringe away from her eyes
she'd crack her whip on my moans and sighs

and amped my lungs like a Mellotron.

My dubbing heart became her holy bomb.

Dissenter

Why so cagey when I wanted to hear
about your language, your homeland, your past?
I kept a notebook to help me remember –
falling behind, then cramming at night.
Your 'class' was poor intelligentsia;
your father Doctor of Philosophy,
later imprisoned as a dissenter.
You never once volunteered his story,
hardly aware of its cultural currency
in the liberal West. I coaxed you for more,
over cake and cappuccino. 'Excuse me,
it is hard to understand this properly.
My father became non-person. Dissenter
is a man who cannot feed his family.'

A Toast

You want me to drink cognac like a Russian –
to knock it back in one, and stomach fire.
I sip and hold and roll it round my tongue.
It isn't *kick* I want, my sweet. It's flavour.

The Chinks

That pow-wow just after our second date –
it felt almost like you were giving feedback
post-interview, when you flatly announced,
how, despite some boxes I don't tick,
there was attraction. Let me drink to that –
however short-lived it would prove to be
for you. Today, I found an early text –
the most emotive thing you ever sent me,
announcing how my touch had melted you…
You'd nowhere to store that heat. My worth
diminished with each flaw I showed you.
To maintain a chrome of drive and discipline
you kept your feelings hidden. Like your teeth
when you smiled: those tiny chinks between.

Song for a Little Child #1

Don't reach for me
with that angel smile
or call me Daddy
when we've played a while.

Your mother frets
to see your heart
push out green shoots
when hers cannot.

Gifts

There's two kinds of gift, according to Dante.
One reflects the tastes of the receiver;
the counterpart projects, as if to say,
this, a part of me, I offer you to share,
so I might grow in you. Imagine there's a third:
the gifts we secretly buy for ourselves,
though telling gift from gift is no less hard
than trusting them to speak up for themselves.
From me to you, then: Omar's Persia;
Turner's paintings, stirring light and storm;
and music for the dancer and the dreamer.
From you to me? To make the type of man
you need: a shirt and tie, crisp as any other;
and *Instinct*, endorsed by David Beckham.

Technique

Back and forth, you like it back and forth.
I weave and work at it for all I'm worth,
but my hips on yours always revert to circles
that come to nothing, however long their cycles.

The Tease

Challenge: reward! Your hook-line on the date site.
The challenge, it suggests, might be your values
(which it's careful not to fully state)
whilst the reward, let's presume, is you.
Of course, you know I'm only teasing;
my ploy when your facade of self-esteem
soars above the praises I can sing.
I know how things are rarely what they seem.
I've handed you the pills you take to sleep.
I've seen the knife-edge you're walking still,
alone, without a safety. My tease is cheap.
Let me snatch it back, and if you're able,
tell me once again (I swear I'll weep)
how Russian girls are the most beautiful.

Song for a Little Child #2

Don't slap my face
with that wicked laugh
when I hold you close,
or play too rough.

Take care, take care –
our ties are broken
should your mother fear
I'm not 'The One'.

The Poet

after Pushkin

Until Apollo grips his scruff
and makes him squawk up blood,
a poet 'gurgitates his fluff
for prizes chipped from wood.

His cosmic Stratocaster's dumb;
his inner life's on sertraline;
of all the world's most useless farts
he is the sparest of all parts.

But once the scorching god stokes up
and rings his ear canal with riffs,
the poet's lungs are breathing deep
on air that chars his synapses.

Each touted shortlist leaves him numb;
he terminates his Facebook page,
and will not smarm or clap his hands
before the Go-To girls and boys.

Like Apollo's Black & Decker
his mouth is champing up its teeth,
until his Twitter profile's scattered
to Homer's beach, to Lear's heath.

The Lover Exiting a Chagall

Her lover stays on longer every night
and when he leaves he kicks the long miles home
and texts her images from every street,
as if he were the eyes and ears of love
and she the judge and jury of the night.

Omens reaffirm the path he strides;
feuding cats bunch tense in hedges,
headlamps chase shadows into copses
and pipistrelles are moonlighting across
a Chagall dreamscape of high slanted lofts.

A beast will reek an entry on this nocturne
of suburbs scented blossom-petal white;
its yeoman belly rasping against earth,
lengthening its fangs against trip-lights,
or alligator-shuffling into dark.

Its phantom itches in his fingered texts
and makes the letters feral on his pad.
'Barsuk!' vibrates her phone from dimming sleep,
but 'nonsense', she replies, 'this England now
is only foxes, taxiing their fleas…'

Poet to Crowd

after Pushkin

Piss off! This outmoded poet
is choking on your trending shite.
Go celebritize your preening vices;
the lyric voice can't syringe your ears!

You're 21 grams underweight.
For all your bannered mainstreamed blah,
from ancient then to rolling now,
the pitchfork mob has been your law.

Go decorate your slavish arses:
from your malls and overpasses
someone sweeps your branded trash.

But having had to quit their service
at altar and at sacrifices
aren't they your priests who shovel ash?

Not for pundits or reviews,
for sponsors or for column inches:
this poet's lit potassium Muse
sprays bon mots like angry finches.

The Dream

You're dancing into the Goodwin fountain.
Snaking through each climbing tine of water,
your blue summer dress clings closer,
almost dissolves, revealing how lean
and strong you are. Body-waving,
your lifted arms draw down the light;
water tongues your feet. The scene is set.
You're a Pushkin debutante, waiting.
I don't hold back. Groomed and fully dressed
I shatter through each rising, falling
column, and take your hands. Spinning,
you waltz us through the liquid excess.
Today, I'm everything you want of me.
You might even say you love me.

Epicurian

After ham cooked in peaches and honey,
then cognac, you're in the mood for passion.
My heart races as something burns in me –
my ulcer. And this yearning indigestion.

Your Russias

'When we go to Russia', you'd say, 'when'.
Your photos of St Petersburg fanned out
in front of us: your voice calm, certain
as you named each fountain, statue, street.
Classical, European – your ideal Russia.
Or those snow plains where you'd shoot and ski –
wild Russia. Not Moscow, where your brother
can't afford to rent – another divorcee
sleeping in his car; where your ex-husband
writes formal demands to your professor
that the daughter he never met be returned
as 'property of the Russian Federation'.
This isn't the country on your screensaver.
You'd rather hang yourself than return.

Song for a Little Child #3

When you grow up
will you still know
why you wouldn't sleep
till I crooned to you

how the owls, the moon
flew down to sing
your Russian name
and then took wing?

Enigma

My lack? Enigma. So that's the problem.
The cultivated absence I call 'the blank'
in you. That won't yield, or give, or rhyme –
your flat refusal of any re-think.
'You are telling me nothing new', you'll say,
as you return each knife in your kitchen
to its rack. Turning on me briskly,
you won't hear another plea spoken –
and won't offer a conciliatory word.
Remember the first time we made love?
As I forgot myself, I leaked the word
you really couldn't bear to hear me say,
and so you tensed and twisted from me. Love,
which one of us, then, gave most away?

Work

'It will take a soldier to win my heart',
you tell me – shooting a well-directed look.
I'm glad I got your verdict on my art:
'Forget it', you say. 'Concentrate on work!'

Holodets

I'd been yarning you about my childhood
in the seventies. In Yorkshire, offal
was often on the menu. 'Peasant food'
I called it: liver, kidneys, heart. So, that single
Christmas we spent together, you made us
your father's favourite, Holodets: meat jelly.
When we asked the butcher for pig's trotters
he winced, but yielded two for free.
Back home, you boiled them for the gelatine –
added the garlic and tiny scraps of beef
and left it to chill. You made a mountain
of the muddy-looking stuff. Hating waste
you gave me boxes to take home. I have to laugh:
you dumped me before I acquired the taste.

Song for a Little Child #4

Just make your way
to your mother's bed
where once I lay
as you called and cried.

You're not too old
to climb back in:
your mother's cold
now she's moving on.

The Singer

after Pushkin

Were you there? He crooned to the oak –
love-struck, in his funeral shift.
When wheat froze stiff under morning mist
and tractors coughed before their work,
            were you there?

Did you see him in his cloak of leaves,
love-whipped, dampening his whistle;
a slug-trail on his cheek, a thistle
in his hair, snooking in his blues,
            did you see?

Did you sigh when you heard him wheeze
the scratchy vinyl of his love?
When you passed him later in the wood,
his eyes like pissed-on embers;
            did you breathe?

After Mandelstam

Don't speak.

Forget
the bird,
lover,
prison.

Day looms,
lips part;
needles
shiver
in pines.

Recall
a wasp,
a lodge,
an ink-
stained box.

Forest
berries

unpicked.

Cazique

'Some months ago Sir Gregor MacGregor, a person of whom we do not choose to say all that we think, induced a number of persons, chiefly Scotch, to emigrate to a settlement which he gave them to understand was formed, and in a flourishing condition, on the Mosquito coast near Honduras. The most deceptive statements were published respecting the country for which these poor people were thus induced to relinquish their homes: it was described as a land flowing with milk and honey, abounding with all the good things of life to such a degree that a man was sure to make his fortune in a very short time.'

The Guardian, 25 October 1823

'And, while he was anxious to play down his heroic exploits on the field of battle, he was rather less modest about the title by which he wished to be known: His Highness, the Cazique of Poyais.'

Roger Cook's *Ten Greatest Conmen*

Ethos

Slowly, I parted ways with honesty.
            There were too many temptations. Lies
open doors; lies are higher currency.
            After one conversation, I can guess
which brand a person has a taste for:
            distortions they eat as a regular meal;
white lies they suck on, secretly, or
            denials they save, like liqueurs, for special
occasions.
                        There are many arguments
against plain speaking: insistence invites
            opposition; or kneejerk judgements
which take a lie or two to put to rest!

            It's so difficult to make truth conform
to people's expectations, or agendas.
            My conversion is cause for alarm;
believe me, I don't expect your applause.

'A Hard Headed Woman'

Save me from gold taps and glass floors;
from the converted barns, kirks and manses;
save me from old debts and younger women;
from luxury packages at the Ritz-Carlton;
save me from tailored suits;
from crafted shoes and crocodile wallets;
save me from Saabs and Jags;
save me from personalised numberplates
and impersonal 'liaisons';
from solicitors, accountants;
save me from my hip flask;
from Talisker and Drambuie;
save me from buttering the town planner;
the councillor, the Laird;
save me from studio bedrooms
with a view of the sea;
save me from carefully executed
business suppers;
from *How to Win Friends and Influence People*...

Save me from knowing what to say,
and when to sign,
and how to unsay and unsign.

Save me from pills;
free me from my Range, my display bookcase;
free me from the first million I made
and the other people's savings I lost;
free me from changing my name and running;

from spiritualists and Jehovah's Witnesses;
and going door to door
with the look of a starved whippet;
give me back the kittens;
give me back your mum's potato salad;
give me back those two years in the caravan;
your flowerbed,
and the first killing we made restoring that barn.

Give back our fisherman's cottage in Portknockie;
that long winter
when the waves leapt over the harbour wall,
wrapping us, for a breath,
in ice and salt
where the love came true in my mouth.

‘For Shame of Doing Wrong’

My father treated everyone
as fools – until they proved him wrong.
‘Robin’, he’d say, ‘you can have
these sweeties, or this ten bob note’;
and if I let my hunger choose
he gave me neither out of spite
or something hidden behind his eyes.
Years, I tried to follow his lead,
only, I couldn’t find my street,
my house, the key to my front door,
and I was running widdershins
as the scene rewrote itself –
never quite appearing to find
the kernel of its story
or the plot, and draft by draft
tall houses divvied into flats;
cinemas aged to bingo halls;
the pubs I haunted shed their names
like bankrupts on their final chance.
I gave up looking at my wake
and never did the decent thing
however sweet and gloopy-eyed
love was – until I chanced into
the way you sized me up and smiled.
My father robbed me of the fool
we need to give ourselves to love:
I let you down and down, into
a ward you nearly couldn’t leave,
but listen to me now, I’ve come
to carve my sins onto this stone
not even I can crawl from under.

Calling Card

I'm one part Satan,
two parts Crow, and several parts
boy – lost so long, now,
down the bottom of this well,
the eye gone blind in the sky.

‘Natural Mystic’

You were working the till in some fashion warehouse
and despite the airhead flaunt of the place,
something in your smile struck me as natural,
so I asked you out. Of course you said no.

I came back every night for three more shifts;
and on the fourth, went home,
drank a bottle of Teacher’s and dreamed this:

All the cliffs of England
were dissolving like an Alka-Seltzer
into an acid sea where serpents swam.
I turned and ran inland,
but no-one in the cities would listen
and when I returned to the failing cliffs
I looked into the sea
and saw one bright face. Of course, it was yours,
and so I stooped and reached
and scalded both my hands pulling you free.

When I woke, I painted
my dream with an airbrush
powered off the pressure of an old tyre.

I showed it to you that night.
When I asked you if it was the vision,
or my sheer persistence that changed your mind,
you only smiled your smile.

Dear Daddy

I'm still waiting at the gate, remembering your beard.
It smelt of smoke and fish. Why did you never smile
when you came home late? I want to go running
on the sand; I want to jump out of a tree into your beard
and scream pretend scared. You can tickle my nose
and sing where's your Ziggy gone. Roast me some chestnuts;
wrap me in pink ribbons. You're the empty side
of the wardrobe; a bottle of brandy Mummy leaves
half full. Promise me sauerkraut and belly pork, a sip
of stout from your thimble. Your not being here
is cod liver oil without malt. Let me stay off school;
feed me medicine that tastes of strawberries;
give me that extra half hour before bed, I'm cold.
I want to name the horses again, hold hands down
the long green alley. I'm scared all the butterflies
will turn into wasps. Come meet me at the gate.

The Hose

When lonely is a bulb
bleaching ceiling and walls,
I exit for the street.
My sister and me
crept home on nights
as cold as this:
Mum might be Mum,
or HER; no food or drink
in the fridge, just lipstick,
mascara; and piss
in bottles, labelled
and sealed.
I'm bad news, it was in
the milk I suckled on…
It's in my finger joints
when I wake in hotels,
vomit and ouzo
on my pillow
and the nightmare
of my hands
around my mother's throat,
gripping like a fool's
who tries to stop
a screaming hose
at the neck.

'Ziggy Stardust'

Once upon a time I was Ziggy's apostle
and learned to be a man who went too far.
If I'm in the zone, I can scam anyone.
How smart they are is nearly irrelevant:
it's their character you're playing, not their brains.
Listen, you've no idea how dull it is
since I lost the glitter. I want it back.
I'm the fog over the bathroom mirror.
The juice has drained out of me, the current.
I'm afraid of what I need to switch back on.
I see it when I look at Sally's husband.
There's a man who likes to make decisions.
Punctilious, but not punctual himself.
Not above a bit of melodrama –
bringing his two bairns to my house
when he thought I was giving Sally
something extra. Can't say I blame him.
There's a man who's always looking forward.
The man without a past, Sally calls him.
He'd nothing but a chair when they married.
Now his name's on half of everything she owns.
It's a shame we're not going into business.
Blokes like George make the game a pleasure.
It's a banana and strawberry smoothie
when you taste what you've taken from them.
A ploy with George would raise my Ziggy.

Iago

I follow him to serve my turn upon him.
– William Shakespeare, *Othello*

I was doing a renovation job
for this professor of Education
          who wanted
a second home for him and his third wife.
He had this manner of talking down from high,
like he owned a monopoly on thought
          and feeling.
Well, I can nod along with anything.
I know exactly which angles to trim;
where to cheat on foundations and joists
          in ways that
only reveal their craft when I'm long gone.
          I can smirk
as I'm drilling my scams into the beams
or secreting them like woodworm larvae.
I like to think of that man looking up
the trading name I'd shed like gloves; dialling
          the number
that triggered the flat-line of a dead end.
          It's simple:
I'm a kind of landslip employed by God
to rock the castles on the hill of smug.

A Killing

Now o'er the one half-world
Nature seems dead, and wicked dreams abuse
The curtain'd sleep…

– William Shakespeare, *Macbeth*

I dreamed I was strapped
into the back seat
when he braced his foot
on that motorway,
drunk, and aimed
his bumper at a bridge.
He no longer believed
he could outrun
his deeds: that litany
of ticking forgeries
I'd coaxed this
tiny-town solicitor
to validate
with his backward-
sloping hand.
I heard him sob out
every crime: each spot
against his daughter's
pony club dreams.
Property development!
He couldn't cruise home, now,
to any life his wife
could tidy up around
each day, and smile.

'Kicks'

How you get your adrenaline flowing now…
– Lou Reed

Marion,
that time you wouldn't
let it rest
        I stiffened
in the driver's seat,
        wedged
the pedal
        and charged
the ramp
of that humpback
        bridge.

When we touched
        road again
we hit a rink
        of ice
and the steering
dissolved
in my grip.

That was
the loneliest gap
        in my breath.

We bounced
        and tumbled
and lucky for us
rolled
the hard six.

‘Children are the only ones who blush…’

It started with that waiver
I needed you to sign.
I stooped an inch
into the door,
squeezed a tear,
and watched
it fall onto my boot –
just so.
I blinked and stared
and eyeball floaters
were tiny punctures
in my light.
You held me, then,
and signed away
what claim you had
on my filthy money.
Back in the Jag
I smiled
and made ‘Caution’
and ‘Give Way’ signs
fast-forward
to the point
of no regret.

The Serpent

I'd left
the game,
and the lives
I broke.
Between Dundee
and Leeds
I woke
from doze
and a dream
of bailiffs
pulling my plugs.
The train
leaned into
a perfect,
dawn-reflective
curve,
and I turned
to admire
the snake
of my getaway.
Light was flaring
off each
carriage window
so I imagined
a domino slither
of re-booting
thoughts –
circuits ticking
through system
restore.

‘A Ghost Will Come’

I’ve been troubled by ghosts since I was a kid,
but only in that limbo-trance between
dreaming and waking:
my mind alert; my body paralyzed;
my fat tongue squirming in its prison
until I wake, cussing
and swearing at the dark;
waiting for the light
to bleach my second sight
and straighten my thoughts again for work.

One dream followed me around for years:
from city to city, house to flat,
my mother would be in
my room. Slowly, she’d comb through drawers;
rifle my pockets, diary, wallet,
or spit into my gin –
whispering to herself
until I gulped awake
on words that made me choke:
guilt and grief fizzing into relief.

Do you remember that night of heavy rain
I woke at 3 a.m., pickled in sweat
and certain someone else
was knocking at the window to get in?
I told you it was a wicked spirit
exiled from the house,
but that was half the truth.
I scratched ‘Jehovah’
above each door;
burned a sprig of sage and held my breath.

For two years I'd chosen to live alone
in an egg-box flat along a tram route.
Every morning at 6.00
I'd wake to a swelling vibration
that wired my bed-head directly to the street.
Once, a little before this
I dreamed about a ghost
so lonely and tired
he climbed into my bed
and slept like someone spent after a shift.

I scouted that flat again, years later,
and thought I saw him at the window,
sipping from a hip flask.
It reminded me of my father,
home from sea, another week to go
before he came to ask
my forgiveness for
all our days he wouldn't
be around to count.
He left us nothing but an empty lighter.

The dead trespass on my awareness
like tears blubbing paths across a blur
of condensation.
They seldom speak, but if a bold one tries,
the words are back to front, slurred,
or simply random.
I often dream of falling
and when I hit the ground
I hear the sound
of children's laughter crowding on the landing.

Sometimes, all I 'see' is an absence in space:
a daub of colour floating by my bed,
dimming into black.
A crouching figure, with a dirty face,
might be an overcoat hung on a doorknob
when I finally wake.
The alphabet soup of the drifting mind
stirs strange figments: often
hinting at a vision
it fails to quite assemble in the end.

But I've traded on it as a medium.
Of course, you'll hear more sense from a sceptic
than many who turn
an ounce of this gift into a tidy sum.
If there's one I regret, it's this trick.
I'd set about to learn
the smell of each client's need,
but I had no gift
for balm or comfort
when it came to ventriloquizing the dead.

I'd send people away feeling more alone,
more abandoned than they felt before;
their business unfinished
with doubt; their grieving hardly begun.
In this fairground house of buckled mirror
I would end up as lost
as them; until I broke.
Furies of debt and hurt
mouthed judgment in a court
with no exit, unless into the dark.

I tried and tried, but couldn't make it work.
Does that surprise you, after all my twists,
after all my stories?
One night, a message startled me awake.
I'd dreamed a soft weight on my chest,
a purring in my ears;
like a cat I loved
back to reward me
for this one honesty.
A small press to the wound, mostly undeserved.

‘Dum Dum Boys’

Wearing that tight England top
and ugly, stony-faced pissed
at 11 in the morning
he leads a Brindle Mastiff –
the sort that could go either way
at the slam of a car door
or a kid across the street.
Next up, the beast skitters free
and is eyeing other dogs –
yappy, scrappy pups on leads,
or faithful mutts with putty brows.
Mothers and their at-home men
are pressing Gary as to what
he’s going to do about his beast.
All this lad can muster is a curse
as his unfaithful friend strays into
the crossroads, then the main road,
until Shannon from the flats
coaxes it into her arms.
‘You’re a wanker’, she tells Gary,
‘you don’t deserve an animal’,
but Gary is too far gone,
a wanker sod, lost and stropping,
not daring a bid for his pet,
but unable to walk away.
So a phalanx is building
of mothers and their mothers,
and Gary, Gary’s on a loop,
fronting up and backing down,
and ‘who d’you think you are’,
he barks, ‘fuck off fuck off fuck off’.

Moses

If a grifter understands
how most folk con themselves,
there always will be some
he can't help on their way.
Christmas week, lunging home
through takeaway fug
in a binging city,
this bloke tapped my shoulder
like pressing my on-switch.
He was built like a navvy,
with the eyes of Moses
flickering in and out
of his wounded glare.
He wanted me to know
he'd fought for this country –
which he didn't call 'his'.
Now he sleeps behind bins
at the back of the uni
if porters don't sweep him
under the bypass.
He'd been to St Mary's
to queue up for soup,
but they'd turned him away
because it was Wednesday…
He sighed out that part, then
said he didn't know
why he did this to himself,
so I asked if he'd tried
to write it all down.

He only said this:
‘The words aren’t my friends…’
On the backwash of that
he walked into the path
of some chundering rahs –
and raised both his arms
and said, ‘look at me;
at the state I’m still in.’
He could bring down the hail
to rap on our eyes.

Edmund the Bastard

...wherefore should I stand
In the plague of custom...

– William Shakespeare, *King Lear*

At wedding receptions
I'll stare into space
as speech after speech
is scrolled from the heart.
When lovers lean close
or mothers well up
I'll feel as remote
as a Hezbollah cell,
and nothing will bloom
but heartburn or cramp
and a lengthening strain
under my ribs.
I grow to expect
you to enter, stage left,
point a finger at me,
knowing full well
I'm taking the piss
when I sit at this feast
with cold meat of boredom
inside my vest...
So I haul myself up;
walk into the street
to slacken my belt
and wonder just where
I'm welcome tonight.

Merry Men

'Yea, on thing greves me', seid Robyn,
'And does my hert mych woo;
That I may not no solem day
To mas nor matins goo.'

– Robin Hood and the Monk

Three ciggie-gaunt and hoody-garbled blokes
are stood around three four-packs of cheap booze.
They have a skanky dog with balls like eggs:
it's off its lead and circling their camp,
and when I draw up close to try and pass
they scold the mutt in slurring, throaty grunts.
The tiny hackles rise along my spine;
my fingernails are sharp inside my fists;
there's a limbo of pure tension as I pass
and four pairs of eyes drill into my back.
I count like someone diving, holding breath,
and when I hear a ring-pull shoot its froth
I turn towards the dog-shit bin, and spit.

‘Badlands’

The drunk by the cashpoint
would rather be sleeping
but his leathery
sweetheart gobs volley
after volley of abuse
into his face. He has to
wince himself erect,
stagger, then push her
square on both breasts,
so she falls, back through
the stages of life
and onto her knees.
She claws herself up
and the moves are repeated
expressing something
ending in puke.
The city’s comeback
is a posse of lads
crossing from Walkabout
and cheering them on –
a scent of *Lynx Africa*
spiking the air.

Logos: Speeches for Two Occasions

That's the fuckin' art of becoming somebody who people can pin their beliefs and their dreams on.

– Irving, *American Hustle*

i.

Are the games we play really so different?
What would you do in the name of survival?
Dress above budget to make an impression?
Amp up the grades of those exams you bungled?
File off the burr of your wherever accent?
Doctor your interests, the place of your schooling?
Miss out the fact that you dropped out of uni?
Claim as your glory the work of a colleague?
Inflate your status by name-dropping others?
It seems to me, now, we serve the same mistress –
and this is the code we have to adhere to:
you need to get creative if you want to level the field.

ii.

You can't make a sum unless you invest one.
If your bait is too big, no-one will trust it.
It has to be small enough to believe in,
but just ripe and firm to make the mouth water.
Whatever it is, you have to present it,
and make sure it doesn't blow up or spiral.
Ideally, don't play with more than one target;
take your time choosing, and learn to spot someone
who needs you to help them push for promotion
to a league just above their natural level.
If you follow these rules, things will run smoothly:
the more noises of caution you sham, the more they'll want to play.

Short Order

The woman at Bukowski's bar
tells me my eyes are jaded –
the colour of tea leaves, stewed.

On the street outside, I stoop
to pluck a daisy from a crack –
its sunny eye blotched with exhaust.

Five O'Clock Shadow

In my father's shaving mirror
my pupils are a shade too black –
and leaking into the iris.

I try to smooth away the bags,
but skin always reverts to type –
sallow as mackerel, smoked.

‘The Secret Sharer’

When I find myself lost between stations,
unravelling nowhere, west north east,
I start to think about who I’d call
my people. They are mostly no-shows
no-one would speak for, or champion;
half-cut and drooling asleep on trains;
lonely blokes on the ends of platforms
who receive no replies, no acknowledgements
from those they reach out to, or recognise
in passing. I can feel them close by:
thickening women in station bars
waiting for men who never remember
to exist. Their extra time is ticking out
as they drink themselves far into helpless.

The Flash

After I'd frittered everything away
I collapsed alone in a one-bedroom flat.
I drew the blinds against each day, and never
let the windows breathe. A rash of mould
spread down the condensation on my walls.
I let it be as I sealed myself in;
hoping it would somehow latch onto me
and eat away my past, my guilty face.
One Thursday evening, my landlord called
and was appalled by how far gone it was.
February. The lowest ebb of the year.
It snowed through the night and the best part
of the following day. All my secrets
felt exposed and cued up for judgement,
so I walked up towards the lonely common
where I knew the snow would fluff its quilt.
The tiring limbs of crusted trees
held a creaking stillness just in place.
I crunched and steamed through deepening white
and when I reached the lip of rising ground
I saw it: almost whiter than the snow,
an instant between heartbeats – a tree
like bony lightning forking into sky.
When my eyes adjusted back to prose
I heard the shuffling photographer cough,
her tripod offset. I thanked her then
for fixing that bright second in her flash,
and when I crashed into my bed that night
I slept with every window gulping wide.

Pumayyaton

On the main street
he's on his knees:
cheeks porous,
stubble like salt.
He's sculpting a collie
out of petted sand;
delicately carving
and grooming the face –
a little wounded,
but loyal, true
behind the eyes.
He makes his stall
a softening place
in Monday morning,
where citizens
in starchy threads
huddle in close
and relent
from blanking.

After Lorca

my daughter
winter moon bowl left out

a basement flat no garden
my skewed smile by your bed
you send me new directions
it empties me to read
  all night across your city
salt-gritted roads glowering stars
shame is gunning for me
with your mother's tired eyes
  last month the roof blew down
each slate I laid was yours
I shiver in this portakabin
pull the curtains closed

split moon broken bowl
my daughter

Friday's Child

That bag lady, waking
to November
on some peeling city bench
is coughing blood.
Her dog-smelling hair,
sandy at the roots,
is draping a face
dirty with bruise.
Sweet cider will not
soften the affront
of Akeba, Hair and Beauty,
or Reeds Rains,
any more than it loosens
her fusing joints.
Some manageress
is lighting up
in a shop doorway,
sunlight bannering
her Hugo Boss suit
and salon-sculpted wave.
She inhales esteem
through her Samsung Galaxy
and purses it out
in kisses of smoke.

'Raging Bull'

I'm sitting in the house again, alone,
but silence isn't going quite to plan.
John is on the street outside, incensed,
launching into a frantic kind of walk
and clutching at his temples with his palms.
He makes it twenty yards, then swings around,
and soon he's back at Linda's window, close,
pressing his dirty mouth up to the glass,
crying 'Please, please, please, please, please…'
He's a bull dying of a broken back
but Linda isn't conjured from the dark…
The upstairs curtain twitches only once,
and there is tiny Liam looking down
at the father who never quite looks up.
I'm sitting in the house again, alone,
but darkness isn't going quite to plan.

My Stomach is Eating Itself

I took too much for myself
and never gave anything back.
The tuneless citizens here
run down on heel-dragging feet
and Class 2 mobility scooters;
they browse the closing-down
high street, or tap in job apps
on the crashing People's Network.
I came here to trump temptation –
to let the place tame me with beer
and TV takeaway nights.
My stomach is eating itself,
mucosa by mucosa. I trudge home
with the same overdraft of life,
jolt off the train in the dark,
damp sandbags in my shoes.
This is my daily atonement
along the central reservation.
Rubble piles by the canal,
greying like apples left to rot.
My bored eyes film into gauze.
Someone has hung a banner
from the overpass, announcing
that Calum is thirty today.
Everyone who passes under
is counting the change of the years,
and they know they've been cheated.
This time the crook isn't me.
I'm dissolving into shadow,
and the acid and spleen
in my guts. I crunch another pill,
and punch the clock in my chest.

I'd Like to Be Elsewhere

or somebody other;
one of those cons
who get out of gaol,
no home to go to,
who end up in a cave
or an air-raid shelter;
the parole officer
turning up flustered
for ten minutes' chat
and boxes to tick.
I'd like to disappear
with only a bible
and my father's hip flask
topped up with the last
of the Islay malt;
drink one sip a day,
until my skin changes
colour, and my scent
and debts dissolve.
Under a scrap pile,
dirty and angular
as a mountain of skulls,
there's somebody else,
somebody better;
a watercress shoot
shouldering grit.

Regret

Robin,
I wouldn't break,
wouldn't cry,
not when the order came
for my eviction,
or when bailiffs
hammered my door.
Only when the vet
sank the needle
into our dog,
whose smell
you'd always
complained of;
who ran amok
and killed my chickens
(each carefully named)
and who whined
with such need
when blood
squirted from his vein
did what glue me together
begin to dissolve
and pearls
appear at my eyes
like a sweat.

‘The Motion’

Doctor, is there a name for this sickness?
My lazy eyelid has started fidgeting,
and it’s spread to the flesh under my tattoos.
Reflux napalms my oesophagus
and a foul-tasting bile climbs up my throat.
Migraines cut out my right field of vision;
contracts read like Satanic Esperanto.
I’m forgetting crucial information:
passwords, pin numbers, noms de plume.
Blood revs a getaway bike through my heart
and I reel like a man at 8,000 feet.
On every job I’m a soul caught short.
Toilets are my restorative niches
where I empty my bowels of myself.

Lions

in my dreams
and panthers,
cheetahs,
lurking muskily;
somehow
not scenting me.
I never stop
fearing they will
as I suck
my own sweat
back into my pores.
There's only
a flimsy tent
between me
and their skin-
stripping breath.
In this dream gazebo
an Iraqi boy
shelters with me –
my twin.
I give him
a potato
black from fire.
He bites deep
and thorny weevils
bleed from the crack –
itchy black crosses
against
my name.

Iago (ii)

'That hustling rictus, Blair
is still brokering deals,
and small fry like me
are branded non grata…'
I picture myself,
revving my spite in the pub,
hushing the small talk
until the bar chief
looms in close to say
'this is a family place…'
Somehow I can't tame
or better throttle myself –
I'm a bowling jack
launched down a flight of steps –
hollow, cast-iron steps –
and folk glare and wince
at every point I gong.
I listen to myself,
spewing an apology,
as if it could make amends
for how a runaway rant
can spoil a halloumi salad
or a witty exchange
about a new exhibition
or a literary prize.
When the gallery
doesn't nod into line,
never raise your voice:
that wrecking ball you swing –
catch it between your teeth
and swallow it down.

Homo Superior

I don't hold with those who say
Bowie dropped his masks in the 80s.
The *Let's Dance* man with sun-kissed hair
and platinum-selling smile
was as artful as anything
previous. True, he blew out smoke
and told the press this was simply
him – but I never sucked it in.
The age demanded a broader
appeal: he bought all the jackets
required – until his edge got lost
in hooks and over-production. See,
he'd built it up and sold it all,
just like he'd promised us he would.

The Man in the Iron Mask

I've run at her wall fifty times or more.
I said, Mother, Mother, where is my father?
Are those his coat and shoes by the door?

She said, your father isn't worth the wait;
your father broke the compass in his heart
and he traded it in for a tub of bait.

I said, Mother, Mother, I have his wallet;
when is he coming back to collect it?
I have his watch, his birth certificate.

She said, your father was swept overboard;
he woke up not knowing what he was for.
He pawned the key to his own back door.

Mother, I comb his thick hair on my head;
walk with the same twist in my tread;
when I smile his smile, my mouth is crooked.

She said, your father slept like he'd had a stroke;
his liver burst into his own blood;
his one good lung was black with smoke.

But Mother, I wear his face like an iron mask;
he's the black beetle shell around my thoughts;
I tighten his screws onto my cheeks.

She said, your father didn't leave a crust;
when we made you, his cock was rudderless;
he'd even steal back the sweat from his balls.

Dear Daughter

I know about the breakers that keep rolling
like boulders bursting through tissue-paper screens.
I brought them on. They flush the length of cruisers
                    forty miles from port.
Snatched like barley inside a harvesting wave
                    a sailor must learn
to graft some iron onto tendon and bone.
At sea it's that, or make out like a feather
                    off a seagull's arse.
It was two years before my first desertion:
a day before your mum went into labour.
                    After my third flit
the navy kicked me into an army prison.
                    It was half rations;
a cell with broken windows and a bucket;
                    snow, and some things worse,
                    shovelled in my bed.
I pictured your toes; made my head a bunker,
and locked my tongue inside until my discharge.
The choices we steer become our own weather.

Robin's Dream

All I had was a clock,
a mattress on the floor,
a bottle of vodka
and a bag of weed.
I was dossing down
in a musty terrace
with holes in the floor
and dream-rats
crawling in my sleep.
I was nobody's then;
and nobody's problem.
I'd taken a drink
and a long, dirty toke
and was falling fast
through a tunnel of swirl
into a garden
of sinking fountains
and one public clock.
The hour-hand raced
like a radar on speed,
holding my gaze
until it formed a mask
with a fiery mouth
that sucked each beat
from my ticking heart.
I woke throwing up,
and back in my room
the wall-clock had stopped
at quarter to three.
From that day on
I was wearing its face.

'Myself Am Hell'

I'm perfectly aware how dead and black my eyes can look.
I have run over small animals in a great big Jag.
I have coerced uncertain lovers to drive a great big Jag
down country lanes, and they have run over small animals
and cried. I invested my second wife's marriage settlement
into a business I broke, and when the bailiffs came knocking
I left all the debts to her. I have not reformed myself,
and have subjected those closest to me to my most
self-indulgent moods. I made half a million in six months
and spent it all in one. I have deceived, and forged what I lacked,
and brazenly bribed all manner of upstanding obstacle.
I drove my business partner to a place where suicide
felt like the only way for him to wash his conscience clean.
I tend to abandon those who will not follow me blind.
I am deaf to anyone who lovingly advises me
against my worst excesses. I have tendered false promises
to my own darlings, and to the children of my ex-wives.
Don't listen to me; I don't have your best interests at heart.
I have no shame. I will be talking to you. You will feel
I am part of your life. You will think all our plans are shared,
but you are just temporary, and I am turning left
at the junction and dissolving into a bigger picture.
I am ambivalent about the social contract. I expect
some of you are too, but you don't vocalize. You,
with your carefully Facebooked, perfectly airbrushed lives,
and your quiet expectation that we should all contribute
to the cause of self-interest under cover of practised hugs.

Some days, I long for someone to turn to me, simply,
and say, 'you are a very nice man', but not often enough
for me to make any serious changes to my breath,
which smells of cigars, and Scotch rotting through a dead pig.
I am by no means a charming and casually adjusted
citizen of liberal views and immediate appeal,
but I have presence and a rare ability to persuade.
Moloch and Belial coach me in my unasked-for dreams.
If you still feel you can save me, you are wrong. If you think
all I want is to retreat into a thickening forest
at dusk, and forget my name amongst the loneliest birds,
then you are precisely the kind of person with most to fear.

Cazique

Nothing I say is entirely
untrue. I wasn't like the boys
with blackheads, or the boys with brass.
When bigger kids would flatten me,
or when I couldn't nod to sleep
my father told me stories
until the night-time lost its edge.
'Robin', he used to say, 'we come
from the flower of the thistle:
way back in the long Tay River
of our blood is the man they called
Rob Roy: debtor, rebel, outlaw
of the glens…' If Dad was drunk,
or darker-tinged and wounded
from my mother's practised taunts
he told me our true ancestor,
his and mine, was Gregor MacGregor –
self-named Cazique of Poyais…
I fell in love with that word, Cazique,
though I couldn't find its meaning
in any book my father owned.
It broke the shackles in my brain:
just thinking it or speaking it
made me taller, other – simply more.
The man I later read about –
veteran, explorer, confidence-
trickster – the stylish crook who made
a brazen fortune selling bonds
to settlers in a republic
little more than mud and flies –
he was the dream-song of myself.

My father often told me this:
folks are stupid when times are good
and hope breeds fools like beef draws flies…
I've had my share of boom and bust,
and now the times have bottomed out
I'm the Cazique of Mexborough –
mucky St Helena of my mind.
I have a plan and all I need
is half of everything you own.

Robin to Marion

i.

  Do you remember
fireworks igniting sunset?
  High-rises sucking
their gigawatts from the grid
as our last tea-lights guttered?

ii.

  All over Whinmoor
air-bomb repeaters frightened
  dogs straining on leads –
the aftershocks triggering
a volley of car alarms.

iii.

  Our room vibrated
when bass-driven Suzukis
  paused at the crossroads –
a police helicopter
beating the air up above.

iv.

We woke around four
to somebody sobbing
outside in the dark.
No-one arrived on the scene
to set their world back to rights.

v.

Come morning, pigeons
landed on our neighbour's roof
and skied down the slates
like angels repairing light
flickering in the gutters.

vi.

Sensitive aspens
had a soft touch with the wind.
It blew empty cans
to scuff our shining puddles
down long streets, from then   to gone.

Pathos

Coughing up my ashy breath
I fight against the urge to shout
and stamp against the creaking cold.
I wince again, recall my sins.
Between the dark fields and the house,
custodian of deepening snow,
I linger on. Don't call me in,
I'm orphan now. Sleeves and knees
are stiffening with cakes of ice;
the old man's socks I used for gloves
are lost in tunnels that I've dug.
My streets are empty as the moon,
curtains closed as sealed-up hearths.
I stop the traffic and the world
and lay down on a snow-white road.

There was another snowed-out road;
traffic and the whole world stopped,
windows rouged like little hearths
and streets unprinted as the moon.
I was digging tunnels in the drifts –
a pair of football socks for gloves,
mint cake wads of snow gone stiff
on sleeves and knees. My mother
forgot to call me in, so I stayed
and pioneered a spit of snow
between the houses and dark fields,
forgetting all my chores. I stood alone,
up to my thighs in creaking cold
and worked my courage up to shout,
signing space with all my breath.

Notes

Officer / Zipped File

The sonnet sequence should be read forwards, whereas the tanka sequence ('Zipped File') is intended to be read backwards, commencing after sonnet 13. The intention is to create a loop.

Holodets

This dramatic sequence tracks the relationship and breakdown of communication between an unknown British poet and a Russian immigrant. The sonnets and epigrams are addressed to her, and the songs to her infant daughter. The sequence is also interspersed with loose versions of Pushkin poems. These marry a 19th century Russian romanticism with a homely and contemporary Northern English idiom.

Cazique

The sequence is in the voice of a small-time conman who believes himself to be the descendant of the great 19th century confidence trickster, Gregor MacGregor – the self-titled 'Cazique of Poyais'. Several titles are taken from songs of the 60s and 70s, especially those by artists who undertook changes of image or identity. Poems in italics are in other voices – one in the voice of his daughter, and the other in the voice of his ex-wife.

Acknowledgements

A version of *Officer* was first published as a pamphlet by Longbarrow Press in 2007.

'The Poet' was first published in *Millstone Grit* (Antiphon Press, 2016).

Special thanks to the following for their invaluable feedback and encouragement: Matt Black, Michelle Bowen, Ray Hearne, Karl Hurst, Brian Lewis, Marianthi Makra, Fay Musselwhite, Ruth Palmer, Jamie Thrasivoulou, and Dr Aled Ganobcsik-Williams.